WH S

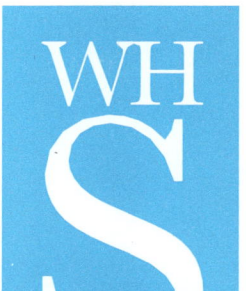

NATIONAL TESTS
practice papers

FOR THE YEAR 2005

English
Levels 2–5

practice papers

AGE
10–11
Key Stage 2

Acknowledgements

The Publishers would like to thank the following for permission to reproduce copyright material:

'The Postman' by Jon Stallworthy, from *Root and Branch*, Chatto & Windus
The Borrowers by Mary Norton, J M Dent, a division of
The Orion Publishing Group
Postage Stamps by L N and M Williams, Puffin Books

Every effort has been made to trace all copyright holders, but if any have been inadvertently overlooked, the Publishers will be pleased to make the necessary arrangements at the first opportunity.

First published in 2005
exclusively for WHSmith by
Hodder Murray,
a member of the Hodder Headline Group
338 Euston Road
London NW1 3BH

Text and illustrations © Hodder Murray 2005

All rights reserved. Apart from any use permitted under UK copyright law, no part of this publication may be reproduced or transmitted in any form or by any means, electronic or mechanical, including photocopying, recording, or any information storage and retrieval system, without permission in writing from the publisher or under licence from the Copyright Licensing Agency Limited. Further details of such licences (for reprographic reproduction) may be obtained from the Copyright Licensing Agency Limited, of 90 Tottenham Court Road, London W1T 4LP.

Authors: Christine Moorcroft and Ray Barker
Series editor: Louis Fidge
Illustrations: Willie Ryan

Impression 5 4 3 2 1
Year   2006 2005

Printed and bound in Spain

A catalogue record for this title is available from the British Library

ISBN 0 340 88858 X

> NOTE: The tests, questions and advice in this book are not reproductions of the official test materials sent to schools. The official testing process is supported by guidance and training for teachers in setting and marking tests and interpreting the results. The results achieved in the tests in this book may not be the same as those achieved in the official tests.

Contents

Introduction
The National Tests: A Summary   iv
How to Use this Book   vi
Insights from Previous Tests   vii
Setting the Tests   viii
Advice to Give to Your Child   ix

Reading Test
Reading Test Booklet   1
Reading Test Questions   7

Writing Test
Longer Writing Test (Non-fiction)   17
Shorter Writing Test (Fiction)   21

Spelling Test   25

Answers
Reading Test   27
Writing Test   31
Spelling Test   32

National Curriculum Levels   33

Introduction

The National Tests: A Summary

What are the National Tests?

Children who attend state schools in England sit National Tests (also known as SATs) at the ages of 7, 11 and 14. Those at ages 11 and 14 are taken at the beginning of May. Those at age 7 can be carried out at any point during the year, as chosen by the teacher. Children in Wales may take the same tests at 11 and 14. All children may also sit optional tests in the intervening years – many schools have chosen to adopt these tests.

The results are used by the school to assess each child's level of knowledge and progress in English and Maths at Key Stage 1 and English, Maths and Science at Key Stages 2 and 3. They also provide useful guidance for the child's next teacher when he or she is planning the year's work.

The educational calendar for children aged 5–14 is structured as follows:

Key Stage	Year	Age by end of year	National Test
1 (KS1)	1	6	
	2	7	KEY STAGE 1
2 (KS2)	3	8	Optional Year 3
	4	9	Optional Year 4
	5	10	Optional Year 5
	6	11	KEY STAGE 2
3 (KS3)	7	12	Optional Year 7
	8	13	Optional Year 8
	9	14	KEY STAGE 3

Timetable

The Key Stage 1 National Tests have so far been carried out in May but, from the school year beginning September 2004, teachers will be allowed greater flexibility as to when they test the children and which tests or tasks they use. Key Stage 1 tests are now based on teacher assessment and can take place at any point during the year as chosen by the teacher.

Key Stage 2 tests take place in one week in May. All children sit the same test at the same time. In 2005, the test dates are **Monday 9 May to Friday 13 May**. Your child's school will be able to provide you with a detailed timetable.

Key Stage 3 students will sit their tests on **3–6 May 2005**.

Introduction

Levels

National average levels have been set for children's results in the National Tests. The levels are as follows:

LEVEL	AGE 7 (Key Stage 1)	AGE 11 (Key Stage 2)	AGE 14 (Key Stage 3)
8			
7			
6			
5			
4			
3			
2			
2a			
2b			
2c			
1			

- BELOW EXPECTED LEVEL
- EXPECTED LEVEL
- ABOVE EXPECTED LEVEL
- EXCEPTIONAL

Results

Your child's school will send you a report indicating his or her levels in the tests and the teacher assessment.

The school's overall test results will be included in local and national league tables, which are published in most newspapers.

What can parents do to help?

While it is never a good idea to encourage cramming, you can help your child to succeed by:

- making sure he or she has enough food, sleep and leisure time during the test period;
- practising important skills such as writing and reading stories, spelling and mental maths;
- telling him or her what to expect in the test, such as important symbols and key words;
- helping him or her to be comfortable in test conditions, including working within a time limit, reading questions carefully and understanding different ways of answering.

Introduction

How to Use this Book

The purposes of this book

- To prepare children for Key Stage 2 National Tests in English by giving them practice, so that they will be familiar with the form of the tests they will take.
- To help parents to judge their children's progress in English.

The practice tests

This book includes practice tests on Reading, Writing and Spelling (Levels 3–5).

Answers and a marking scheme are provided at the end of the book.

The Reading Test (Levels 3–5)

15 minutes are provided for reading the booklet, during which no writing is allowed (cut this out). 45 minutes are allowed for answering the questions.

Most children take the Levels 3–5 test. The Reading Test comprises a variety of texts – perhaps non-fiction, fiction and poetry – testing reading strategies across a range of genres. There will normally be a link or a common theme between the passages.

The questions set will require four different kinds of answers.

- Short words or phrases. Usually one mark is allocated for each correct response.
- Longer answers – one or two sentences. Usually two marks are allocated for these answers as they require more understanding of the text.
- Detailed explanations of opinion. These involve a more personal approach. Up to three marks are allocated.
- Multiple choice – where several choices are given and the child should choose the correct one. Single marks are allocated for each correct response.

Incorrect answers are given a zero score, and no half marks are awarded.

Although some of the questions will have a "right answer", all children will express their responses in a different way. When marking the questions, look for the content of what has been written and not just the quality of the writing, grammar, etc.

The Writing Test (Levels 3–5)

At Key Stage 2 children's writing is assessed through two Writing Tests:

- a Longer Writing Test (45 minutes);
- a Shorter Writing Test (20 minutes).

Children should be allowed time to plan their writing for both tests, which they should not do one after the other.

In the National Tests, the **Longer Test** is assessed for: **Sentence structure and punctuation**, **Text structure and organisation** and **Composition and effect**. The **Shorter Test** is assessed for **Sentence structure, punctuation and text organisation** and **Composition and effect**.

Sentence structure and punctuation focuses on the use of variation of types of sentences, clarity, purpose and effect, and on grammatical accuracy and punctuation.

Text structure and organisation focuses on organising and presenting whole texts effectively, sequencing and structuring information, ideas and events, constructing paragraphs and using cohesion within and between paragraphs.

Composition and effect focuses on imaginative, interesting and thoughtful writing, writing a text which is suitable for its purpose and for the reader, and organising and presenting a text effectively.

Handwriting is assessed in the Longer Test, but is not assessed in this book.

Spelling is assessed in a separate test.

The mark schemes each year are specific to the tests; new level thresholds are set for each year's tests to ensure that standards are maintained each year.

Assessment of children's attainment in National Tests depends on the judgement of professionals. For the purposes of this book, a simplified system of marking is used based on Content (composition and effect) and Grammar and structure (sentence structure, punctuation and text organisation).

Guidelines to National Curriculum Levels provided on page 31 should be regarded as a rough guide only.

Introduction

Children's writing is assessed in two ways:

- Purpose and organisation: for example, if the child is asked to write a letter, has he or she set out the letter correctly? Does he or she show an awareness of the audience of the letter? Has information from the original text been used?

- Grammar – style and punctuation: for example, is the style of the letter correct? What level of sentences is being used? Is the writing clear? Does the use of punctuation help the writer to communicate his or her meaning?

The Spelling Test (Levels 3–5)

10 minutes are allowed for this test.

A passage containing gaps is provided. You are also provided with the complete passage on page 32 – the words being assessed are in **bold**. Make a copy of this page for ease of use. Read the passage to your child and pause at each of the 20 missing words to allow him or her time to write the word in the space.

Insights from Previous Tests

Every year, an analysis of the performance of children in the National Tests is produced. The main points in this analysis can be useful when helping your child to attempt the tests in this book.

Below are some of the recommendations made:

Reading – Encourage your child to:

- look across the text to see any patterns, for example, a sequence of events, the use of illustrations;
- generalise from two or three instances;
- explain the organisation and layout of texts;
- identify the purpose of the text and the audience for whom it was written;
- explore the precise meaning and effect of words.

Writing – Encourage your child to:

- use commas to mark clauses in longer sentences;
- check the use of commas in lists;
- revise the use of possessive apostrophes (for example the dog's bone) at all levels;
- pay attention to the ending of the writing;
- choose carefully when and where to start a new paragraph;
- organise paragraphs to make and develop points effectively.

Introduction

Setting the Tests

A relaxed approach is best. If you feel anxious, your child will sense this and might not concentrate or perform as well as he or she could.

Work in a quiet place where you and your child will not be distracted. Choose a comfortable, secure environment in which to do the tests together.

Before beginning the tests, cut out pages 1 to 6 and staple them together to make a reading booklet. You may also find it useful to make a copy of page 32 as your guide for the spelling test.

Your child will need a pencil and, if possible, an eraser. If you do not have an eraser, ask your child to cross out any mistakes made.

Provide some extra paper – although some answers need to be completed in the book.

The tests in this book are modelled as closely as possible on the "real thing" so pupils will not be surprised by the test format. However, parents can help with the pressure of the tests by using the material in this book as a resource for teaching and learning. Do not just sit your child down with a test and tell him or her to "get on with it"; share the experiences, questions and discussion that arise. Try sitting one yourself!

- Encourage your child to read the texts carefully.

- Point out that there are different types of questions, for example those which give a choice of answer (one of which your child should tick) and those which ask for a written answer. When writing an answer your child should write in complete sentences, where possible.

- Talk about each of the questions and what your child will need to think about for the answer.

- Tell your child to have a go at answering every question; and to leave any questions he or she cannot answer, and go back to them at the end.

- Stick to the time limits – but do not insist that the entire test paper has to be completed in one go.

- Give immediate feedback.

- Mark the work with your child, praising positive points as well as pointing out things which are not correct. Be positive about achievements!

- Look closely at how the incorrect responses can be corrected, what needs to be learned or changed and how this can be done realistically. It is useful to list just two or three things which need to be done or learned before the next test session.

- If you have any questions, ask your child's teacher.

Advice to Give to Your Child

- Keep an eye on the time! When you are practising, spend a little longer at first, but aim to become quicker. Remember: you will not be given any extra time in the real test! When your teacher says, "Put your pens down" – that's it!

- Which question is worth the most marks? Spend more time on that question – but not too much more time.

- Look at how many marks are allocated. Try to make that many points. If there are 2 marks, make 2 points (and back them up with proof). This will keep you looking for information and writing until the end.

- Don't ignore the help you are given on the paper. The questions tell you what to think about. Use these prompts as a plan for your own reading and writing.

- Underline or highlight the key points. You can write on the test papers and it is helpful to do so. You have 15 minutes of reading time to start so you can begin to get ideas and remember where key points are to be found.

- Make your notes before you start to write. The aim is not to fill in as many sheets in your answer book as possible. You only get the one chance so think about what you want to write before you put your pen to paper.

- When you write your answer, write in sentences – don't just copy your notes on to the paper.

- Don't be afraid to cross things out and write them again. It is important to be neat but it is more important to say what you really mean.

- Write in paragraphs (you could leave a line between them) as this makes your work easier to read.

- Use quotations – but not huge chunks! It is best to quote short phrases and single words.

- Good luck!

Reading Test
Reading Test Booklet

Sending a Letter

Contents

Introduction 1

Postage Stamps 2
Non-fiction

The Borrowers 4
Fiction

The Postman 6
Poetry

Introduction

Writing and sending a letter may seem like a very ordinary thing to do, but this was not always the case.

In this booklet we shall look at aspects of sending a letter in three different ways:

- from an information text;
- from a story in which a letter plays an important part;
- from a poem.

You have **15 minutes** to read through these passages.

Reading Test

Postage Stamps

(From *Postage Stamps* by L N and M Williams)

The world's first postage stamps were issued by Great Britain on May 1, 1840, and came into use on May 6. Their introduction was due to the efforts of Rowland Hill, at one time a Birmingham schoolmaster, who produced a plan to reform the Post Office. He succeeded in interesting Parliament in his plan, which was adopted in 1839.

Before 1840 the postage on a letter was usually paid by the person who received it, and, as the postal rates were very high, some people, especially the very poor, used to dread a visit from the postman. Postage was charged according to weight: a letter weighing two ounces (about 55 grammes) sent from London to Croydon cost two shillings and six pence (twelve and a half new pence).

The high charges were caused by inefficient working of the Post Office, and Rowland Hill's plan showed that letters could be sent all over the country for one old penny each (less than one penny today), and still enable the Post Office to make a good profit. So as to make the sender of a letter responsible for the postage, Hill suggested that it should be paid in advance, by sticking a stamp to a letter.

There were two values of stamps: 1d (one old penny) and 2d, both showing the head of Queen Victoria. They were printed in London in sheets of 240 stamps, and were 'imperforate' (having no perforations). Although over 150 years old the Penny Black and the Twopenny Blue are not very rare, but are in great demand by collectors.

Two years after Britain had introduced postage stamps to the world, a private postal service, working in New York, issued a stamp, the first to appear in the Western Hemisphere. Other issues by postmasters in the United States were made in the next few years and in 1847 came the first stamps for use throughout the USA, with two values: Five Cents Brown, showing Benjamin Franklin, and Ten Cents Black, showing George Washington.

In the meantime, the Swiss canton of Zurich brought out two stamps, four and six 'rappen'. Then from Geneva came a curious stamp: it was in two halves. If one wanted to post a double weight letter the whole stamp had to be used, but for an ordinary letter the stamp was cut in two and one half affixed. This stamp is known to collectors as 'The Double Geneva'. A picturesque issue from Basle (also spelt Basel), in July 1845, showed a dove in flight. Known as the 'Basle Dove', this was the first multi-coloured stamp, the dove being embossed in white on a red background with pale blue corners.

The Borrowers
by Mary Norton

The Borrowers are tiny people who live in the spaces behind your skirting boards and are responsible for all those things you can never find because they 'borrow' them. They like to be secret, but Arrietty decides to write a letter to make contact with another group of Borrowers.

Pod threw down his borrowing bag. He stared at his wife.

'What's the matter?' faltered Homily, looking from one to the other.

'She was in the night nursery,' said Pod quietly, 'talking to that boy!'

Homily moved forward, her hands clasped tremblingly against her apron, her startled eyes flicking swiftly to and fro. 'Oh, no –' she breathed.

Pod sat down. He ran a tired hand over his eyes and forehead; his face looked heavy like a piece of dough. 'Now what?' he said.

Homily stood quite still; bowed she stood over her clasped hands and stared at Arrietty. 'Oh, you never –' she whispered.

'They are frightened' Arrietty realised; 'they are not angry at all – they are very, very frightened.' She moved forward. 'It's all right –' she began.

Homily sat down suddenly on the cotton-reel; she had begun to tremble. 'Oh,' she said, 'whatever shall we do?' She began to rock herself, very slightly, to and fro.

'Oh, mother, don't!' pleaded Arrietty. 'It isn't so bad as that. It really isn't.' She felt up the front of her jersey; at first she could not find the letter – it had slid round her side to her back – but at last she drew it out, very crumpled. 'Look,' she said, 'here's a letter from Uncle Hendreary. I wrote to him and the boy took the letter –'

'You wrote to him!' cried Homily on a kind of suppressed shriek. 'Oh,' she moaned, and closed her eyes, 'whatever next! Whatever shall we do?' and she fanned herself limply with her bony hand.

'Get your mother a drink of water, Arrietty,' said Pod sharply. Arrietty brought it in a sawn-off hazel shell – it had been sawn off at the pointed end and was shaped like a brandy glass.

'But whatever made you do such a thing, Arrietty?' said Homily more calmly, setting the empty cup down on the table. 'Whatever came over you?'

The Postman

Satchel on hip
the postman goes
from doorstep to doorstep
and stooping sows

each letterbox
with seed. His right
hand all the morning makes
the same half circle. White

seed he scatters,
a fistful of
featureless letters
pregnant with ruin or love.

I watch him zig-
zag down the street
dipping his hand in that big
bag, sowing the cool, neat

envelopes which
make *twenty-one*
unaccountably rich,
twenty-two an orphan.

I cannot see
them but I know
others are watching. We
stoop in a row
(as he turns away),

straighten and stand
weighing and delaying
the future in one hand.

Jon Stallworthy

Reading Test
Reading Test Questions

Sending a Letter

On the following pages, there are different types of questions for you to answer in different ways. The space for your answer shows you what type of writing is needed.

Short answers
Some questions are followed by one line.
This shows that you need only write a word or a phrase in your answer.

Several line answers
Some questions are followed by two or three lines.
This gives you space to write more words or a sentence or two.

Longer answers
Some questions are followed by more than three lines.
This shows that a longer, more detailed answer is needed to explain your opinion.
You should try to write in full sentences, where possible.

Multiple choice answers
For these questions you need to do no writing at all.
You need to choose the best word or group of words to fit the passage and put a tick next to your choice.

Marks
The number under each circle in the margin tells you the maximum number of marks for each question.

Please wait until you are told to start work on page 8. You should work through the questions until you are asked to stop, referring to your reading booklet when you need to.

You will have **45 minutes** for this test.

Reading Test

These questions are about *Postage Stamps*.

In questions 1 to 4, choose the best number, word or group of words to fit the information in the passage. Put a tick next to your choice.

1 The world's first postage stamps were issued in

| 1839 | 1840 ✓ | 1845 | 1847 |

2 Before this date, postage was paid by

| the very poor | the sender of a letter | the person who received the letter ✓ | the Post Office |

3 Posting a letter was very expensive

| because of inefficient working by the Post Office ✓ | because there were two values for stamps | because letters were not very heavy | because stamps were "imperforate" |

4 After Britain, the next place in the world to produce stamps was

| Washington | New York ✓ | Geneva | Basle |

5 Below is a summary of events in the history of the postage stamp, but they are mixed up. Number each stage in the correct order.

3	Stamps come into use
1	The British Parliament adopts Rowland Hill's plan to reform the Post Office
2	1d and 2d stamps are issued
4	First private postal service in the Western Hemisphere is started

Reading Test

6 Write down TWO things we learn about Rowland Hill's life from the passage.

Hill was at one time a Birmingham schoolmaster, who produced a plan to reform the post office. He succeeded in interesting parliament in his plan which was adopted in 1839.

[2 / 2]

7 Give ONE reason why the poor used to dread a visit from the postman before 1840.

~~because the postal rate was very high~~ because they had to pay

[1 / 1]

8 Explain TWO ways in which Rowland Hill made a difference to the way that postage was paid.

Letters could be sent all over the city for one old penny, still enable the post office to make good profit

[2 / 2]

TOTAL 5

Reading Test

9 Draw lines to match the stamps to their place of origin.

Twopenny Blue	Basle
Ten Cents Black	Zurich
Four and six "rappen" stamps	USA
A multi-coloured stamp	Britain

10 Explain what was curious about "The Double Geneva".

because the post stamp was cut in halfy, othat of the post was not heavy, they would only put a halfue stamp and if it was heavy they would cut both of them

11 What was the purpose of designing the stamp in this way?

_____
_____
_____
_____
_____

12 Label this diagram to show that this stamp is a "Basle Dove".

Blue corners
Dove
red background

TOTAL
8

These questions are about the passage from *The Borrowers*.

13 How do you know that Homily is upset from the way she acts? Find TWO pieces of evidence from the passage.

She threw her hands are trempting. she is moaning and she is faltered

14 What TWO pieces of evidence can you find to suggest that Pod is also worried by the situation?

his face looked heavey like a piece of dough. he is talking to arltey sharply

15 Explain what Arrietty realises about why her parents are reacting in this way. How does she try to reassure them?

that they are only frightened not angry her parenth looked concerned about what she's along but she doest understand the reaction.

Reading Test

16 Describe how Arrietty finds and shows her parents the letter she has received.

just she couldn't find the letter it had slid round her side to her back but at last she drew it out very cold crumbled

3 / 3

17 To whom did Arrietty write her letter? Who did she ask to deliver it?

her uncil hendreary wrote it and the boy deliver it

✓ / 1

18 Find TWO pieces of evidence from the passage to suggest that the Borrowers are very small.

they are tiny people who live in spaced behind your skatingboards ✓

2 / 2

19 From the passage, what can you tell about the three characters from what they say and how they behave?

*pod seems more calm than his wife.
homily is trying to hide her emotion anxety. calm, trying to find out why her parents are acting like that.*

3 / 3

TOTAL 9

12

Reading Test

These questions are about the poem "The Postman".

20 Where does the postman go to in the first verses of the poem?

he is going from doorstep to doorstep and stooping sows — 1/1

21 What is he actually doing?

delivering posts. ✓ — 1/1

22 The poet describes him as someone who "sows". What kind of person normally sows?

a farmer — 1/1

23 To what does the poet compare the letters in the second verse of the poem?

He is comparing the letters with the seeds — 1/1

24 Why are the letters "featureless"?

because we don't know whether the post has bad news or good news — 2/2

25 Why does the writer describe the postman as zig-zagging down the street?

because he is delivering posts to different houses. — 2/2

TOTAL 8

Reading Test

26 "envelopes which
make *twenty-one*
unaccountably rich,
twenty-two an orphan."

Why are the words "*twenty-one*" and "*twenty-two*" printed in italics?

the post a postman might read what is on the envelopes.

3

27 Find THREE words in the poem which describe the movement of the postman as he does his job. Write ONE word next to each dot.

- Zigzaging
- scatters
- sawing

3

28 Explain why the people in the house are

"weighing and delaying
the future in one hand"

when they pick up their letters.

because they are weighing to see if they have a lot of letters and to see if they think that they have good news or bad news

3

TOTAL

9

Reading Test

These questions are about all three texts on **sending a letter**.

29 The three texts were written by different people for different audiences.

Match the text to the audience with a line.
Draw ONE line to each box.

Text	Audience
Postage Stamps	Someone who is interested in making an imaginative picture about an everyday occurrence.
The Borrowers	Someone interested in history who wants information.
The Postman	Someone interested in a fantasy world who wants to imagine how people there would behave.

3

TOTAL

3

Reading Test

30 Some readers may not think that sending a letter is anything out of the ordinary.

Explain why these three passages might change their view.

_____
_____
_____
_____
_____
_____
_____
_____
_____
_____
_____
_____
_____
_____
_____
_____
_____
_____
_____

3

TOTAL

3

Writing Test
Longer Writing Test (Non-fiction)

Instructions

Choose ONE piece of writing from the following:

1. *I felt I must write…* (a letter to persuade); **or**

2. *Number On Window Catches Thieves* (a newspaper article).

Someone is allowed to read through this section with you.

Plan and organise your ideas in the spaces provided.

Spend about 15 minutes thinking about what to write and making a note of your ideas.

You will have a total of **45 minutes**.

I felt I must write…

You read this letter in your local newspaper. You are so angry about what it says that you decide to write a letter opposing this view.

Write your letter. The purpose is to persuade people that the letter writer's view is wrong.

> I don't know what's wrong with the young people of today. All this moaning about bullying in schools. When I was a child it was never bullying just because someone called you a few names or hit you once or twice.
>
> Everyone in school gets picked on for some reason but you have to be strong enough to fight back. If you can't fight back then you must be a weed, that's all I can say.
>
> My child came home the other day with a letter from his teacher saying children have to talk about what is happening to them and that they have to tell teachers. This is just telling kids to tell on their mates.

You should think about:

- how you will start the letter;
- the best way to organise your arguments;
- how to make the points as clearly as possible;
- how to finish your letter.

Remember:

- you are trying to persuade someone to share your views.

You can make notes in this space.

_____
_____
_____
_____
_____
_____
_____
_____
_____
_____
_____
_____
_____
_____
_____
_____

Writing Test

Number On Window Catches Thieves

What story might this newspaper headline be describing?

Imagine you are a newspaper reporter who has to write about the event.

Write an article about what happened. Make it as exciting as possible.

You should think about:

- the sort of information you need to include;
- how you will start the newspaper report;
- the best way to organise your points;
- how to make the points as clearly as possible;
- how to finish your article.

Remember:

- you are giving people information as well as making it exciting for your reader.

You can make notes on page 19.

Writing Test
Shorter Writing Test (Fiction)

Instructions

Choose ONE piece of writing from the following:

1. *A Day in _____ Street* (a description or short story); **or**

2. *The Letter* (a short story).

Someone is allowed to read through this section with you.

Plan and organise your ideas in the space provided.

Spend about 5 minutes thinking about what to write and making a note of your ideas.

You will have a total of **20 minutes**.

Writing Test

A Day in _____ Street

Make up a name for the street. Decide what kind of street it is. Imagine the events of a day in the street.

You should think about:

- buildings and other objects;
- people;
- what happens.

Questions to ask yourself:

- What are the characters like?
- How can I show this in a very short story?
- What are the relationships between the characters?

You can make notes in this space.

_____
_____
_____
_____
_____
_____
_____
_____
_____
_____
_____
_____

The Letter

Imagine that you find this fragment of a letter. Tell the story of what happens and how you explain the mystery.

> Go to the tower
>   You will see
> Beware of the door on the left. It has a magic
>
> Remember what you have learned at school about the power of the owls.

You should think about:

- how you found the letter;
- what happened;
- who was involved;
- how the mystery was solved.

Remember:

- characters;
- the setting;
- how you will begin the story or description;
- what happens;
- how you will end the piece.

You can make notes on page 24.

Writing Test

Spelling Test

The first stamps were _issued_ in May 1840. Rowland Hill produced a plan to change the Post Office and he _succeeded_ in persuading Parliament that this was a good _idea_.

Before this time, postage was _usually_ paid by the person who _recieved_ the letter – a very different situation from today. The cost of postage was very _high_ because it was determined by _weight_ and _according_ to the _distance_ that it had to _travel_. This meant that the very poor used to dread a visit from the postman, _especially_ if the letter had come from afar.

The Post Office was also very _enficiant_ ✗, which led to high charges. Rowland Hill _showed_ that letters could be delivered all over the _country_ for only one penny each.

In order to do this, the sender had to be _responsible_ for the cost of the postage, so _stopping_ people being charged for letters which they did not expect.

The first stamps – a Penny Black and a Twopenny Blue – are now much looked for by _collectors_. In the second half of the nineteenth century, all over the world, postal services began to grow, _brought_ about by the work of Rowland Hill in Britain. _Through_ his example we now have many _curious_ stamps – including a triangular-shaped one from South Africa and a two-part one from Switzerland.

TOTAL
20

Answers
Reading Test

POSTAGE STAMPS (Non-fiction)

1 The world's first postage stamps were issued in 1840. — **1 mark**

2 Before this date, postage was paid by the person who received the letter. — **1 mark**

3 Posting a letter was very expensive because of inefficient working by the Post Office. — **1 mark**

4 After Britain, the next place in the world to produce stamps was New York. — **1 mark**

5 — **1 mark**

3	Stamps come into use
1	The British Parliament adopts Rowland Hill's plan to reform the Post Office
2	1d and 2d stamps are issued
4	First private postal service in the Western Hemisphere is started

6 He came from Birmingham; he was a schoolteacher. — **2 marks**

7 **One** of the following:
Postal rates were very high.
Postal rates were paid by the person who received the post.
The poor could not afford to receive post. — **1 mark**

8 Any **two** from:
All post in Britain cost 1d (one penny) or 2d.
The sender paid the postage.
The postage was paid for in advance.
Stamps were introduced. — **2 marks**

9 — **2 marks**

Twopenny Blue	Britain
Ten Cents Black	USA
Four and six "rappen" stamps	Zurich
A multicoloured stamp	Basle

10 This stamp was made in two separate halves. — **1 mark**

27

Answers

11 It would be more versatile. Double weight letters took both parts of the stamp. Ordinary weight letters took one half. **2 marks**

12 Parts that could be labelled are:
a flying dove
red background
corners (in blue in the original) **3 marks**

Maximum mark: 18

THE BORROWERS (Fiction)

13 Any **two** of the following:
Her hands were "clasped tremblingly" – she was shaking.
Her eyes were startled.
They were flicking to and fro.
She "faltered" when she spoke. **2 marks**

14 Pod "ran a tired hand over his eyes and forehead".
His face looked heavy – "like a piece of dough". **2 marks**

15 Her parents seem very concerned about what she has done and she does not understand their reaction – she has only written a letter.
She thought that they were angry because she had disobeyed them in talking to the boy and using him to deliver the letter.
She comes to realise that they are frightened. She has made other people aware of their existence and this could put them in danger.
She tries to reassure them: "It's all right –" but they are too concerned. **3 marks**

16 She had hidden the letter "up the front of her jersey" – the top she is wearing.
She could not find the letter because it had slipped around the back.
She takes it out and hands the crumpled letter to them. **3 marks**

17 It was written to Uncle Hendreary. The boy delivered the letter for her. **1 mark**

18 Any **two** from: Homily sat down on a cotton-reel – obviously used as a seat.
They used a sawn-off hazelnut shell to drink from.
They "live in the spaces behind your skirting boards". **2 marks**

19 Pod: Seems calmer and quieter than his wife. He appears worn out and concerned about his wife.
Homily: Very much the worrying kind, her actions and expressions all show she panics and cannot hide her emotions, for example she shrieks and nearly faints.
Arrietty: Calm, works out why her parents are acting in this way, but cannot really see what she has done wrong. **3 marks**

Maximum mark: 16

Answers

THE POSTMAN (Poetry)

20 He moves from doorstep to doorstep – from house to house. **1 mark**

21 He is delivering letters – moving from house to house to post the letters through the houses' letterboxes. **1 mark**

22 A farmer or gardener normally sows. **1 mark**

23 The poet compares the letters to seeds. **1 mark**

24 Often the outsides of letters tell you nothing about what is inside them.
Envelopes are often plain. **2 marks**

25 He is moving to and fro across the street in an irregular line. **2 marks**

26 These are the numbers of the houses which he visits.
The italics tell us how the postman might read what is written on the envelopes he is holding. **3 marks**

27 Any **three** from:
Goes   Scatters
Stooping   Dipping
Zig-zag   Sowing
Turns away
3 marks

28 The letters may contain news which is good or bad. This could change people's lives. The people don't know what is in the letters before they open them but they pause and think about it as they pick them up. **3 marks**

Maximum mark: 17

Answers

GENERAL

29 The boxes should be matched as follows: **3 marks**

Text	Audience
Postage Stamps	Someone interested in history who wants information.
The Borrowers	Someone interested in a fantasy world who wants to imagine how people there would behave.
The Postman	Someone who is interested in making an imaginative picture about an everyday occurrence.

30 The factual, information passage tells you why and how postage stamps developed.
The story tells us how it is possible to get into trouble over writing what you think is an innocent letter.
The poem gives us an unusual view of an "ordinary" postman. **3 marks**

Maximum mark: 6

Answers
Writing Test

The following criteria provide guidelines to help you to gain an idea of your child's Writing Level. Each level assumes that the criteria for the previous level have been met.

Assessment of children's attainment in National Tests depends on the judgement of professionals who use a more precise numerical marking system. For the purpose of this book, a simplified system of marking is used based on Content (composition and effect) and Grammar and structure (sentence structure, punctuation and text organisation).

Content (composition and effect)	Level
Is the narrative in the correct form (for example, in an appropriate layout and in the correct person and tense)? Is fiction writing imaginative? Is non-fiction writing clear and does it have a logical structure?	Level 3
Is there an attempt to interest the reader? Is the style or viewpoint maintained throughout most of the writing? Are the criteria suggested on the planning sheet met?	Level 4
Is the tone of the writing maintained throughout? Is the language expressive and effective? Are the vocabulary and language appropriate for the purpose of the writing (for example, the use of technical language, metaphors, similes or comparisons)? Are they suitable for the reader?	Level 5
Grammar and structure (sentence structure, punctuation and text organisation)	
Are the ideas presented in sequence, with full stops, capital letters, question marks and commas usually used correctly? Is a greater range of connective words and phrases used (for example, *next, afterwards, so*)?	Level 3
Are some of the sentences long, with correctly-used connective words and phrases (for example, *meanwhile, however, which, that, who*)? Are conditionals, such as *if* or *because*, used? Do some sentences contain more than one verb or include commas, semi-colons, exclamation marks or speech marks? Are the tense and person consistent throughout? Does the structure of the text add to its effect?	Level 4
Are commas and speech marks used correctly throughout? Is a range of connective words and phrases used? Are punctuation marks used correctly, including brackets or dashes and colons, to separate parts of a sentence? Is the length of the sentences varied to express meaning? Are passive or active verbs used appropriately?	Level 5

Answers
Spelling Test

The words missing from your child's spelling test are those printed in bold below. Read the passage to your child, then read it again, pausing at the words in bold to allow your child to write the missing word in the text. Give one mark for each correct answer.

Maximum mark: 20

The first stamps were **issued** in May 1840. Rowland Hill produced a plan to change the Post Office and he **succeeded** in persuading Parliament that this was a good **idea**.

Before this time, postage was **usually** paid by the person who **received** the letter – a very different situation from today. The cost of postage was very **high** because it was determined by **weight** and **according** to the **distance** that it had to **travel**. This meant that the very poor used to dread a visit from the postman, **especially** if the letter had come from afar.

The Post Office was also very **inefficient**, which led to high charges. Rowland Hill **showed** that letters could be delivered all over the **country** for only one penny each.

In order to do this, the sender had to be **responsible** for the cost of the postage, so **stopping** people being charged for letters which they did not expect.

The first stamps – a Penny Black and a Twopenny Blue – are now much looked for by **collectors**. In the second half of the nineteenth century, all over the world, postal services began to grow, **brought** about by the work of Rowland Hill in Britain. **Through** his example we now have many **curious** stamps – including a triangular-shaped one from South Africa and a two-part one from Switzerland.

National Curriculum Levels

Use the conversion tables below to gain an idea of your child's National Curriculum Level from his or her test marks.

Reading

Non-fiction Reading	
Mark	Level
0–4	Below 2
5–8	2
9–12	3
13–15	4
16–18	5

Fiction Reading	
Mark	Level
0–1	Below 2
2–5	2
6–9	3
10–13	4
14–16	5

Poetry Reading	
Mark	Level
0–1	Below 2
2–5	2
6–9	3
10–13	4
14–17	5

General	
Mark	Level
0	Below 2
1–2	2
3–4	3
5	4
6	5

Spelling

Mark	Level
0–3	Below Level 3
4–9	Level 3
10–14	Level 4
15–20	Level 5

Total marks

Write your child's marks here:

Non-fiction Reading	
Fiction Reading	
Poetry Reading	
General Reading	
Spelling	
Total (maximum 77)	

Approximate National Curriculum Levels for Reading and Spelling

Marks	0–23	24–37	38–64	65–77
Level	Below 3	3	4	5

See page 31 for guidelines as to Writing Levels which do not have a numerical score.

If your child needs more practice in any English topics, use the WHSmith Key Stage 2 English Revision Guide.